I0417706

Lashonna Cargin

Dealing with

OCD

Copyright

04/05/2017

Legal zoom

Introduction

Do you find yourself unable to stop obsessing over someone or deal with individuals or not able to understand your love one you will learn how to do all the above. I wrote this book to help people understand OCD and their loved ones to understand them in know there not the only one going through these things in there live.

Lashonna Cargin Dealing With OCD

-
- **Table of Contents 1**

Chapter 1......................................3

-
- **How   it all started**

Chapter 2

-
- **New   Friends**

Chapter 3

-
- **Big   O Mess..........................5**

Chapter 4

-
- **Getting   out the Situation......7**

Chapter 5

-
- **The   Big Surprise…..............11**
-

Chapter 6

-
- **Getting   Self together............12**

References.....................................14

Dedication.....................................15

Biography...........................**16**

Lashonna Cargin Dealing with OCD
How It All Started
Chapter 1

Lashonna is in the doctor's office with Sage who is a mature Asian women with long black hair. Sage is one of Lashonna friends. Lashonna finds out she has OCD from her doctor Mary a mature older black women with long hair.

Back to the story Lashonna has been depressed over Habakkuk who is light skinned with curly black hair in sexy big eyes. But he doesn't like her. Her OCD tells her that he does. It all started when Habakkuk and Amos who also is light skinned with curly hair. They came over Lashonna house to see Abraham, Because he does music for 1914. Habakkuk would always talk to Lashonna, but he was trying to be her friend.

One day Lashonna an Habakkuk took a trip to Royal Park an amusement park in Ohio. Dinah and Delilah twin sister very mature for their age. One has long hair one has short hair one is tall one is short. Also there is Moss Green who is a young black women that wears a wig and is also chunky. Abraham Lashonna's Brother and his wife is Vashti they also came too.

Habakkuk asked Lashonna to ride on a ride with him and he had won a stuffed animal before he got on the ride and give it to Lashonna and she was so excited to ride with him she forgot and left the stuffed animal on the ride. Lashonna doesn't know that Moss Green liked Habakkuk, because she missed her graduation because she thought they would be together. So one day after they got back from the amusement park. Lashonna and Moss Green got in a fight. Abraham Lashonna brother found out about the fight and told Lashonna"he is not thinking about any of us you need to make you some new friends and move on." What will Lashonna do?

NEW FRIEND

CHAPTER 2

Lashonna meets sage and the others at the same religious place where they both did religious volunteer work. Sage's husband is a tall chunky white man. With short black hair. Her Husband's name is Mark. Mark is from the Midwest one of his friends Paul wants to get married he is a white mature men with no hair and looks very geeky.

So sage goes to the Midwest with Lashonna to met Paul in Lashonna is so excited. So they go out on a date Lashonna and Paul.

Lashonna's OCD gets in the way. She started to look at her drinking glass to check for germs or dirt or food, she checks also the silverware too. Lashonna does this, because her OCD tells her there's something wrong with the silverware and glass and gems are on Paul hand. Then at the end of the date paul wants to shake her hand, but Lashonna want more than just a handshake. So they exchange emails. Sage asked "did Paul email you" Lashonna said "Yes he just wanted to be my friend because he felt so uncomfortable during the date.

Sage helped Lashonna work on her OCD by having Lashonna get fast food and telling her "eat the hamburger and fries if you are still alive in five minutes you are going to make it." Time has pass and Sage started controlling Lashonna by telling her what to do all the time. One day they took a trip to Maryland to visit Lashonna's cousin Professor Violet she is a mature black women with long hair in very thin. She is a psychologist . Lashonna also want to see Aunt Cyan she is a sweet mature black lady with long hair. They both try to help Lashonna with her depression. Aunt Cyan notice that Lashonna wanted to watch a movie but, because sage told her don't , Lashonna didn't either. Aunt Cyan told Lashonna" is that want you want to do or is that what sage wanted you to do? So Lashonna come home Monday, and sees on her phone that Dinah and Delilah are having a gathering Saturday at their house this weekend who will Lashonna meet?

A Big O Mess

CHAPTER 3

Time has passed there is a new guy in town his name is Judas he is a mature

Spanish guy with a receding hairline, and he teaches all of us how to do Latin dancing

that all want to Royal Park amusement park. We all were there except Abraham and his

wife Vashti. A month later we all meet again at Dinah and Delilah's house to play cards

this time. So it's time for Lashonna to leave so she asks Judas to walk her to her car.

Lashonna always parks her car close to the house but someone park in her spot, it was

Judas. Lashonna found out because as they were walking to her car she said "someone parked in my spot. Judas said "I wonder who it can be". Then he hit his key chain and it

beep and Lashonna started to laugh. Lashonna did not know that Judas and Abraham

hang out together and he asked him "where is your sister at"? So Lashonna goes to the

Spanish congregation to help spanish speaking people learn the bible and keep her

OCD busy by learning a new language. Judas started talking to Lashonna at every

religious meeting. Then Lashonna meets a girl name Asparagus she is a young brown

skinned women short hair sometimes she wears a weave. Asparagus become a friend

Just to get close to Abraham after he got a divorce from Vashti . Lashonna's OCD tells

her that she is a good friend to have. Lashonna is blinded by the fact that Asparagus is

using her to get close to Abraham. A few months later when she realized her Obsession

with Judas being. She would talk about him all the time and daydream about them being

married and tell everyone about her liking him, the same thing she did with Habakkuk all

over again. Then a girl name Jezebel a light skinned chubby young women who thinks

everyone wants her, she was so mean to Lashonna would tells her that "no men are

looking at her and don't want her." Jezebel started liking him, also she would come to

his meeting and go over his house trying to talk to him. Lashonna didn't like Judas at

first it took while before she started liking him, but there was a attraction there. Then

another girl started to like Judas her name was Green she was light skinned with weave

and short hair. And her friend Acid Green who was a young black women with glasses

tried to help her get Judas. Fern is a young Asian women with bad acne and long hair

and chunky, and her fiend Mantis who is a young black women with short hair in

chunky. Then two months later Groen put her book to block Lashonna seat at the religious meeting. Goren who is a mature young black that is chunky with long hair.

She would tell the congregation that "Lashonna came there to stalk

Judas " which was a lie. Then Green would talk about Lashonna's hair and how it was

stylized and the things she had on. Then Mantis and Fern would send email to

Lashonna telling her that Judas don't want her and move on, and called her house

telling her these things.

Then a month later Jezebel kept coming to Lashonna's Job. Lashonna 's mother

would tell her she need to "forgive and forget". She does and Jezebel calls her to invite

her to a movie where Judas is going to be there but Lashonna doesn't know he is going

to be there she thinks that she is going to meet some new men. So Lashonna goes

Jezebel she rides with her. Then she gets there in sees Judas talking to another girl and

setting with her. Lashonna doesn't know the girl he is with. Lashonna is so hurt by what

Jezebel does. Two weeks later Jezebel calls Lashonna on the phone in invites her to do

some religious volunteer work. She is being forgiving and she goes. Jezebel tells her

"she needs to stay away from Judas and leave him alone because he doesn't like you."

Lashonna told her " If I knew he was going to be there I would not have went to the

movies with you" Jezebel tells Lashonna after that "OH". Then Jazebel tells "her she is

being tested by all the girls." After two week it takes it toll the emails the coming to the

job and to her religious place and they were not a member of it. Phone calls then

Jezebel wanted her Jacket back since Lashonna borrowed a jacket from her some time

back before all this mess started. Lashonna mom told her "not to go", but she didn't

listen and got in a bad car accident. Abraham Lashonna's father told her "Don't you ever

go back to that Spanish congregation again and don't you ever talk to Jezebel again."

A month later Abraham Lashonna's Brother calls professor Violet to tell her what all happened. Then Professor Violet told Lashonna"are you OK do you need me to come down there, you need to get out of that situation. Then Lashonna talked to Aunt Cyan she told her "you do not need him,let him go" So Lashonna listen to the advice and cut off all her friends except Elisha she is a mature black women who looks Asian she would help Lashonna by telling her that "God don't like all this Drama." Two days later she called her aunt Bernice who is a mature older black women with long hair. Lashonna tells her what was happening in Ohio, because Bernice lives in Atlanta. Bernice tells her" to look in the Bible at <u>James 1:13</u> it says God doesn't test with evil. So the girls are acting demonic in you need to stay away from them because they are bring you down." So What will Lashonna do?

Getting Out The Situation

Chapter 4

Lashonna moves to Atlanta for six months, and cuts off all association with Judas and the girls, because the people that love Lashonna dearly help her see for herself that she needs to move on with her life. And the girls were all in the situation together. In to get out the situation she had to move to Atlanta. Lashonna stayed with her aunt Bernice and Uncle Matthew he is a mature older men with no hair and chunky she stayed up stairs in the gust room. Two month have passed by an Lashonna meets a sister name Verde she is a dark skinned mature older southern lady with short hair. She help Lashonna find a place to live in Atlanta . At the same time all this was going on Aunt Bernice wanted to keep Lashonna on the right track with God so she asked Atarah to be like a mentor to Lashonna while she lived in Atlanta. One day they went out to do religious volunteer work and she talked to Lashonna about good and bad association in how you can get into a lot of trouble in Atlanta because there is so much activities to get into. So she would plan a group of friends to go out to help them see how they can have a good life from following the Bible. One of there names were Mary she is a dark skinned mature black girl. The Second one was Bethany she a dark skinned southern mature girl. The last one was Jael she also is dark skinned southern but a young women. A month later Lashonna calls a friend she meet in Ohio her name is Athalian she is a dark skinned young women who likes to be by herself. She had a lot of roommates and never stayed at a place for two long. Lashonna wanted to hang out with her but, she told her"don't you have some other friends you can be with "Lashonna OCD told her, she was a friend Lashonna was a little confused.

Lashonna has been in the house with a her roommate Salome for five months now. Salome is a dark skinned southern mature women with Bipolar disorder that own her house and rents rooms to sisters. To help pay off the mortgage. Salome kicked out a girl name Herodias she was from Nevada and Salome kicked her out four month along because she thought she would be a bad influence on Lashonna. Lashonna never got to see Herodias so Lashonna doesn't know what she looked like or were she moved to,but before she left Herodias took Salome to court for throwing her out because it was against the contract she sign when she moved.

In the last Month she lived in salome house. One day salome had came back from Spain because she goes there to preach about the Bible. In her head the house is mess but if you have OCD you know the house is clean. But not to Salome's standards she looked around the house trying to find somethings wrong with it. Lashonna Has her aunt Bernice over to check the house the day before she came and she said the house was clean, nothing was wrong with it, Bernice's brain is normal. So Salome blows up on Lashonna because the pillows were not in the place that she wanted them to be. Then salome calls and talks to aunt Bernice and she tells "Salome to be nice and kind about talking to Lashonna about how she didn't like the house because it was not put back the way she wanted it to be. Salome acted demonic and talked mean and nasty to her thinking that no matter what she said she was going to stay at her house. Salome tells Lashonna"Nobody wants you living with them and your mom doesn't want you to live with her." So Lashonna is upset and confused because her OCD tells her everything is clean in alright. So Lashonna call her cousin Adirel in she asks"how much does a hotel cost because aunt Bernice doesn't want me to stay with her. Cousin Adriel is a dark skinned mature women.

So aunt Bernice calls in tells Lashonna" Pack your bag and come home to me, because when I see her I'm going to tell her off for what she told you." So Lashonna pack her bag little by little Salome got a attitude one day, Lashonna came over and told her"don't you have a key just open the door with your key." Out of respect she ring the doorbell. Then Salome tells her that "She is not right to leave the house, because your suppose to be be forgive and forget this happen" Lashonna said you are bad associations for my OCD because you bring me down and I gotta go". Next day she is living with aunt Bernice for a while until Lashonna's mom Sarai comes to Atlanta Three month later Salome lost her job and house so this goes to show you what comes around goes around.

The next week Aunt Bernice and Lashonna,mom and Dad, Abraham had a cook out. When Lashonna's mother Sarai who is a light skinned women this is the sweetest women in the world who will stand up to anyone that hurts her baby. While at the cookout over aunt Bernice cousin Adriel had a talk with Lashonna in she told her " To go back to Ohio to support her mom because, her sister Mercy she is dark skinned older mature women with short hair. Don't do volunteer work or go to religious meeting any more. She said she doesn't have a chance to talk to her mom or go out in do volunteer work with her mother or see her mom and you have the opportunity to do this"
There was a surprise for Lashonna, wonder what is was?

The Big Surprise

Chapter 5

Lashonna was getting a big surprise she found out when she moved back to Ohio that her brother was getting remarried because, Vashti left Abraham seven months ago, and never told Lashonna she was getting a Divorce, the new sister-in-laws name is Sarai

she has the same name as her mom. She is a tall light skinned women with long hair in

very understanding of Lashonna's OCD in try's to work with her to reason right on life

issue.

It's been two months since Lashonna been back and it's wedding time. Lashonna

is excited ,because she gets to wear a pretty red prom dress. And Lashonna fixes her

hair up very nice. The whole family is there they all look alike they are dark, and light

skinned with slanted eyes and big eyes in wavy hair on both sides .Judas were there

Lashonna didn't know it, and he asked Green to dance with him. Lashonna 's cousin

see this in tells her she should be out dancing with everybody so, Lashonna goes out to

dance but when she does she dances with Judas friend Titus who is dark skinned men

with muscles and they dance for three songs. Then she ends up dancing with Amos for

one song then she dance with Stephen with help from her cousin he is a nerdy mature

guy with glasses. And as they were dancing he stop and wants to dance with Sarai.

Habakkuk sees all this and he say" I will dance with you Lashonna they dance for two

songs. After all the dancing Abraham sings a song he wrote for Sarai and they have

their couple dance. They show picture of the process of their relationship which was

nice and has some of the women crying at the wedding Three years has pass what is

Lashonna doing about her OCD?

Getting Her Self Together

chapter 6

Lashonna took professors Violet advice and went to get Professional help in her own state. She went from therapist to another therapist for months, because when Lashonna found one her insurance would change. After searching for six months she found one name Zephaniah this one was great because he specialized in OCD. Zephaniah would use. Exposure and Response Prevention, because it worked he would have Lashonna set in a chair were there was a computer and he would have Lashonna turn it on .Lashonna would have to set there for five minutes. Zephaniah would also have Lashonna set by cleaning product and a glass of water and leave the room for five minutes and Lashonna would pray to Jehovah for help to control her thought in her head. Lashonna never did anything wrong no bad emails, no poisoning people it was all in her head the OCD would have her thinking she was doing all these things.

Next two months Zephaniah has Lashonna test her OCD because the OCD is telling Lashonna that she is writing bad things on pieces of paper, So Lashonna has to set in the room again for five minutes by herself with a pad of paper and a pen. Lashonna being to pray to Jehovah for help to control the thoughts in her head. Once again nothing happened. So Zephaniah told Lashonna to take antidepressant to ease some of the anxiety away. During her therapy for three months she realizes that she need to rely on Jehovah more and have faith that he is going to help her get thought this illness she may have for the rest of her life.

Lashonna family is very helpful through all this mom Sarai is very patient and helps Lashonna reason like normal people. Abraham her father he is tall older black men this in an rocket sciences. He is dark skinned with wavy hair in slanted eyes. He would use Reverse psychology to help Lashonna think in reason like normal people. Abraham Lashonna Brother he helps by putting a cell phone by Lashonna and a tablet by her so she can see that nothing is going to happen and know one is going to let her do anything on their phone or tablet, Zephaniah told her a way she can tell is she did anything in her head was "she could feel herself doing something or someone will find out and let her know but it is all in Lashonna's head."

Lashonna had to stop and think out of all the Therapist, the superior Therapist was Jehovah. The one that knows her inside out and can fix her chemical imbalance that causes OCD. Jehovah loves you unconditionally . You can ask him to take away your tears and negative thinking . by asking him to help you think positive. My favorite scripture is Isaiah 41:13 For I, Jehovah your God, am grasping your right hand,The One saying to you, 'Do not be afraid. I will help you.' Another scripture is Joshua 1:19 Have I not commanded you? Be courageous and strong. Do not be struck with terror or fear, for Jehovah your God is with you wherever you go." The last scripture is Deuteronomy 31:6 Be courageous and strong.± Do not be afraid or struck with terror before them,± for Jehovah your God is the one marching with you. He will neither desert you nor abandon you."±

these scriptures help Lashonna realize that Jehovah blessed Lashonna with a mentor Athalia she is a African mature older women with short hair sometimes wears braids. She goes out to religious preaching work with Lashonna. Also get Lashonna on a diet to eat fruit and vegetables. Doing all this help Lashonna OCD stared to get under control a little bit. By spreading God's message helping people better their life's is the best therapy you can have.

Jehovah has blessed Lashonna with the most power drug of all being an aunt because Lashonna has to get better because she doesn't want her family to see her in an institution were she can not be with them. So her new additions to the family can be proud of her just like she is proud of her aunts.

During this Journey of OCD Lashonna has realized that no matter if you are a Jehovah's Witness you still have good and bad in all religious because no one is prefect, but remember Jehovah has not done anything to you, so she goes to all her religious meetings. If Lashonna get obsessed with a guy and he is not interested she will cut him off because you are going to keep liking the guy. Chose friends that like you and that will build you up, and that will be there even when there is bad OCD days. Only be around people who understand OCD or willing to deal with OCD because you are only going to create problems for yourself. The final thing is to eat right its OK to eat fast food every now in then even sugar but not all the time.

As you can tell I'm Lashonna and this is my story about OCD I hope you liked it and you learn something from it. I hope I was not too. Religious, but Jehovah has helped me cope with OCD my family has help me cope with it too.

REFERENCES

chapter 6 third paragraph NEW WORLD TRANSLATION OF THE HOLY SCRIPTURES

from Jehovah Witnesses

DEDICATION

This book is dedicated to my Mom
and Dad and Aunts who have
been patient in helping me and sticking with me
all the years of my OCD I love you
so much for your advice and help
and Mom and Dad I love you
the most for not giving up
on me and not putting
me out the house.

BIOGRAPY

Mrs walker lived in Ohio since 1978 when she got older in 1989 she got OCD but could not go

to any doctors because she didn't have the money now she can get help. She could not keep a job

in customer service , because a lot of people don't know how to handle OCD they don't

understand it. Lashonna decided to write her first book about her life story to see if it can help

someone with OCD and see the things that trigger OCD. Lashonna is sorry that it is so short

,but she likes to keep things short and sweet in to the point. Lahshonna feels you can't help someone with OCD unless you have it yourself. Lashonna did graduated in 2003

with her family's help her mom help her with English, because she is good in English and her

dad is great in Math. Lashonna mom and dad broke down information for her so she can

understand it like they did when they teach her the Bible. Lashonna has let her OCD control

her whole life but hopefully you or your family member or friend can stop their

OCD from this Book.

www.ingramcontent.com/pod-product-compliance
Lightning Source LLC
Chambersburg PA
CBHW060830290526
45792CB00005BB/1875